MAGNETIC

MEDITATION

5 MINUTES TO HEALTH, ENERGY, AND CLARITY

D1572563

Also by Ilchi Lee

The Call of Sedona

Change

Healing Society

Brain Wave Vibration

In Full Bloom

Principles of Brain Management

Healing Chakras

Earth Citizen

Mago's Dream

LifeParticle Meditation

MAGNETIC

MEDITATION

5 MINUTES TO HEALTH, ENERGY, AND CLARITY

ILCHI LEE

BEST
LIFE

BEST
LIFE

BEST Life Media
6560 State Route 179, Suite 114
Sedona, AZ 86351
www.bestlifemedia.com
877-504-1106

© 2013 by Ilchi Lee
ISBN-13: 978-1-935127-62-8
First paperback edition: October 2013
Library of Congress Control Number: 2013943763

Please understand that this book is not intended to treat, cure, or prevent any disease or illness. The information in this book is intended for educational purposes only, not as medical advice. Always check with your health professional before changing your diet, eating, or health program. The author and publisher disclaim any liability arising directly or indirectly from the use and application of any of the book's contents.

Cover design by Malou Leontsinis
Interior design by David Redondo

Wishing you a healthy, happy,
and fulfilling life

Contents

Introduction

About thirty years ago, twenty-one days of extreme as-
cetic practice enabled me to tangibly experience how
energy operates in our bodies. At that time, I realized
that this world is not only made up of the matter we see.
I perceived my own substance as particles of brightly
shining energy, waving and vibrating endlessly. All the
divisions and boundaries between me and the world
disappeared completely. Then I realized that my energy was the energy of the cosmos and that my mind
was the mind of the cosmos. After that powerful real-
ization, I started calling that vibrating energy "cosmic
energy," which is the substance of all life, including me.
This energy has also been called *ki, chi,* and *qi* by various
traditions in Asia.

I realized that the world of energy I saw at this moment of enlightenment was very similar to the world
described by physicists. When we split matter continuously until we reach the level of elementary particles,
a similar world of energy is revealed. I came to have

a great deal of interest in the nature of the world depicted by modern physics, and, inspired by this, I christened cosmic energy with a new name—*LifeParticles*.

As revealed by modern physics, elementary particles are the smallest components of everything in the universe that the human species has discovered so far. The concept of LifeParticles stresses one thing in addition to the concept of the elementary particles of matter. It is the power of the mind that moves elementary particles, which could also be called *spirit*. LifeParticles are particles containing life energy, which we can experience in a state of pure consciousness.

Since obtaining enlightenment, I have been thinking hard about how I might be able to share my insights so that they are a little more universal and understandable to the public. I would like to express them in a way that fits the sensibilities of modern people. During my quest, I have researched and developed over 300 diverse programs of mind–body training.

Anyone can experience all of this content, but only if he or she is able to feel energy. Unfortunately, many people have been unable to experience this world of energy deeply because their sense for feeling energy was weak. Thus, I have created Magnetic Meditation. Magnetic Meditation is a method designed to enable anyone to easily, quickly, and powerfully experience LifeParticles, the cosmic energy that is the essence of all life, by using magnets.

The study of energy is different from typical academic study because it is not something you can teach or learn through transferring knowledge alone. Each person must acquire a sense of energy through direct experience, as when learning to swim or ride a bike. That does not mean, however, that special abilities are needed. Anyone can feel energy once his or her sense has been developed. It's not much different from feeling warm sunshine or a gentle spring breeze on our skin. Energy actually exists and can be felt concretely.

Energy is obvious to those who feel it, but I was still frustrated that some could not. Then, an idea came to my mind that made me exclaim, "Oh, I've got it!"—magnets.

All living things have biomagnetism—a weak magnetism flows even in our bodies. If you hold a magnet in your hand and move it around close to your body, you'll feel a tingling or electric current. This is because the biomagnetism in your body responds to the magnetism of the magnet. That feeling is similar to the sense of energy we normally feel in a meditative state.

If you use a magnet, you can experience energy quickly, easily, and strongly, even if you have a lot of trouble concentrating. Use a magnet to feel energy, to expand that feeling, to spread it to other parts of your body, and to communicate with other people through energy. You'll find that in that process of increasing your energy sensitivity you naturally acquire the techniques of meditation. Meditation is essentially the ability to concentrate on the "here and now." As you use magnets, your concentration improves and, as a result, your ability to feel energy improves. Feeling energy in the moment becomes meditation.

The ultimate goal of meditation is discovering your true self. No matter what environment you grew up in or what education you received, no matter whether you are old or young, no matter what your profession, your worldly identity is only an extremely small part of what makes you who you are. Within you is a self with power much greater and brighter than you think. If you immerse your body and mind in the ocean of energy that always surrounds you, you will encounter a great, bright, powerful self that is unlimited by any external condition or environment.

Your feelings and emotions change continually depending on your energy state. You feel good and your mind is open when energy is flowing properly within your body. Conversely, you feel bad and your mind is closed when energy doesn't flow well because it's blocked. This also applies to what happens between people. If energy flows well between people, the atmosphere improves; if it doesn't flow well, problems develop. The reason why you may dislike someone seemingly without cause and why you may be attracted to someone without really knowing the reason are both due to the unseen interactions of energy.

Energy is at the source of all phenomena. Many of the physical and mental problems we experience stem from energy circulation and imbalance. Consequently, positive changes happen in our bodies, minds, and personal relationships when we change our energy to restore good circulation and recover balance. When we work to put our own energy into a good state, we become better able to help others actively, enabling them to do the same.

All the Magnetic Meditation training exercises in this book are games for awakening your energy sense and for adjusting your energy balance. Whenever you get the opportunity, try to practice using your body and the magnets in a playful fashion. As you spin the magnets in your hands, try to feel changes in their subtle pulling and pushing forces. Distracting thoughts will vanish, and your sense of life will awaken when you concentrate on such feelings. The biomagnetism of your body resonates with the magnetism of the universe if you cultivate a pure state in which ideas and thoughts have ceased to function.

If you can activate your energy sense so that you can move and control life energy freely, you have achieved a state I call the *zero point*. This state of energy and consciousness is the heart and ultimate goal of Magnetic Meditation. When we achieve zero point, we become free of our distracting thoughts and emotions, our creativity blossoms, and our bodies and minds are healed. We develop magnanimity in our personal relationships, learning to accept those who think differently, and we remain composed, even when under stress. Also, our natural healing abilities are activated to maintain a healthy body.

A big-picture perspective—one of integration, unity, and fusion that allows us to see everything as one—develops in our consciousness when we recover our zero point. Within this consciousness, we develop discernment to see even contradictions in an integrated way, and we become able to use contradictions for creative drive, not as sources of conflict or confrontation. When we recover zero point, our brains also develop an optimal state with the ability to process information efficiently and to find solutions to difficult problems.

As denizens of a digital civilization, you are probably comfortable playing with knowledge and information through cell phones and computers. When your mind is distracted and your heart is troubled, instead of reaching for a digital toy, try playing energy games and meditating with magnets. Playing with magnets for a while, you will find positive changes in your body's magnetic field. When surrounded by healthy, balanced magnetic fields, love, joy, vitality, creativity, and other positive emotions and energies are created. May you become a person who, through Magnetic Meditation, actively changes your own energy and the energy space around you, creating hope for yourself and for others.

ILCHI LEE
Sedona, Arizona, Summer 2013

CHAPTER

1

The Magnetic World

Energy Management Is the Key
to a Healthy Life

Magnets of many shapes and sizes occupy one corner of my office. Some I received as gifts and others I bought myself out of curiosity as I developed interest in magnets. My favorite is a magnetic levitating globe. Lately, I always take this globe with me whenever I give a lecture. It helps me explain the difficult-to-grasp world of energy in a way that people easily understand.

When the globe is in place, it floats magically above the base. This effect happens because of the power of magnets. Inside the stand, below the round globe, are several magnets, and there is one in the globe, as well. To make the globe float, you must find the central point where the forces of those magnets meet. The magnet in the globe pushes downward, and the ones in the base push upward, creating perfect balance between forces. If you lightly touch the globe with your hand while it floats and rotate it slightly, it will continue to rotate on its own in the air.

The globe is able to float in the air because the difference between the opposing magnetic forces pushing and pulling between the globe and stand is *zero*. In other words, the zero point of force has been recovered in this state. Without finding that zero point, you can never float the globe in the air; it will just stick to one corner of the stand and won't move at all unless someone forces it.

Zero point is also what we need in our lives. We need to rediscover a proper balance of energies so that we can glide effortlessly through life, like the globe spinning above the base. But unfortunately, many people have lost their balance, and they are stuck, like the globe out of alignment with the magnets. For years, I have been teaching people how to feel and use energy so that they can improve the quality of their lives. Energy runs through every aspect of our lives—health, emotions, relationships, finances, and almost anything

you can name—so learning to understand and balance these aspects is key to living a happy, fulfilling life. Magnetic Meditation, I believe, is one of the simplest, easiest-to-use methods of energy management available.

I encourage you to ask yourself this: How is the globe of my life turning right now? Unless you work consciously to maintain zero point, it's easy to lose your natural balance and lean or tilt to one side. Magnetic Meditation is a path to self-discovery and a way to reestablish balance in all areas of life.

We Live in Electromagnetic Fields

You are an energetic being. All life-forms on the Earth, including human beings, sustain life by obtaining energy, directly or indirectly, from electromagnetic radiation. This is because the sunlight that maintains the planet's temperature and sustains our lives is electromagnetic radiation. All the food you eat, which is converted into energy in your body, contains energy from the sun. Vegetables take the sun's energy directly through photosynthesis, and animals consume that same energy when they eat grass, algae, or other plants.

The sun emits electromagnetic waves of different frequencies, and some of them reach the Earth. The visible light we sense with our eyes is a portion of those electromagnetic waves. If there were no light from the sun—that is, if there were no electromagnetic radiation—then we would be in such a blackout that the future of humanity, indeed, of all life, and the planet would be unimaginable.

How, then, did humanity discover the existence of electromagnetic radiation? This goes back to the discovery of electromagnetic fields.

Electricity and magnetism had long been known, but they were considered unrelated phenomena until the nineteenth century. At that time, scientists discovered that electricity and magnetism are inseparable forces.

Danish physicist and chemist Hans Oersted observed in 1820 that the direction in which a compass needle points changes when the compass is placed near a wire carrying electric current, revealing a connection between electric currents and magnetism.

Over a decade later, Michael Faraday—wondering whether it might be possible to create electric current in a magnetic field—discovered that if he moved a magnet in and out of a coil of conductive wire, an electric current flowed in that wire.

About thirty years passed before James Clerk Maxwell predicted the existence of waves with both electrical and magnetic properties—in other words, electromagnetic waves—and this was demonstrated through experiment. Later it was learned that electromagnetic waves generated in electrical circuits could be sent or received through an antenna. Technologies that use electromagnetism, such as radio communications and broadcasting, were invented using these discoveries.

Electromagnetism is carried by photons and is divided, in sequence of increasing frequency, into radio, microwave, infrared, visible, ultraviolet, X-ray, and gamma radiation. However, regardless of their length or frequency, electromagnetic waves propagate in a vacuum at the speed of light—fast enough to circle the Earth seven and a half times in one second. Visible radiation is the portion of the spectrum of light detected by the human eye.

Electromagnetic radiation can be created artificially, although it also occurs naturally. Artificial electromagnetic radiation is used broadly in many different fields, including broadcasting, satellite communications, industry, medicine, and science. As a result, we are living in electromagnetic fields created artificially, as well as in the natural electromagnetic field of the sun. Not only has it become difficult to imagine a world without the Internet, cell phones, and televisions, but use of inexhaustible electromagnetism, including for laser treatment, remote observation, remote control, and satellite communications, is making our lives richer and more convenient.

The Earth Has a Magnetic Field

What is the reason why the needle of a compass always points in a set direction? It was reportedly around the fourth century BCE that the Chinese started using a magnetic needle attached to a light reed or piece of wood and suspended in water to determine proper building alignment. It was some two millennia later, however, that the underlying principles involved were discovered.

Thanks to sixteenth-century English astronomer and physicist William Gilbert, we now know that the Earth is a massive magnet. The planet itself is a magnet whose north pole has a south polarity and whose south pole has a north polarity, so the north of a compass, being attracted to the pole that has south polarity, always points north.

The reason why the Earth has magnetism is that hot iron, nickel, and other minerals are contained in liquid form in its interior, and as these are spun slowly by the Earth's rotation they act like a generator.

A magnetic field surrounding the entire planet like

a massive bubble is created by the magnetism generated in the planet's interior. The strength of the Earth's magnetic field was first measured in 1835 by a German mathematician and physicist named Carl Friedrich Gauss. Currently it is measured in real time by many governments and agencies through observatories and satellites because of its importance.

The Earth's magnetic field, although invisible to the eye, can truly be called a planetary defense shield that has an absolute impact on the survival of all life-forms on the globe. If the planetary magnetic field did not protect the Earth from the powerful, high-energy cosmic particles that are constantly streaming from the sun, it would be as if nuclear bombs were falling from the sky like rain. Earth's life-forms and much of its atmosphere would cease to exist.

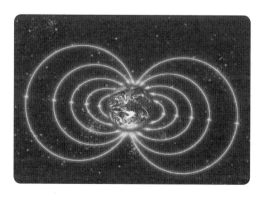

The atmosphere of Mars, which has lost its magnetic field, has continued to decrease due to the effects of the solar wind; what remains is no more than 1/100 of the Earth's atmosphere.

In this way, the Earth is more than just ground and atmosphere. Its unique magnetic field protects and preserves the planet's entire ecosystem.

The Human Body Also
Has a Magnetic Field

All vital activities in living organisms are electromagnetic phenomena created by the particles that compose that life-form. Our bodies deliver and process information and maintain vital phenomena using electrical signals in all of our organs, including our brains, hearts, muscles, and nerves. The speed by which information is transmitted through our nerves is greater than 400 kilometers per hour. It takes about 0.01 second for a signal to travel from the foot to the brain. The nerves are able to deliver information this rapidly because they change all information into electrical signals first.

The current of electricity that develops when information is transmitted along and between the nerve cells of the brain is called "brain waves," and a graph of these brain waves is called an "electroencephalogram." The electrical activity that occurs with the beating of the heart is amplified and recorded graphically in what is called an "electrocardiogram."

Where electricity flows, a magnetic field always forms, so biomagnetic fields form in and around the human body. Although they are very weak, these biomagnetic fields can be measured in real time and imaged, thanks to the developments of science and technology.

You don't see it, but around you right now an energy space, your own biomagnetic field, encloses your body. All life-forms, not just humans, have these subtle bio-magnetic fields.

This unseen biomagnetic field is protecting you, just as the Earth's magnetic field protects the planet's living inhabitants. Our biomagnetic fields change moment by moment with our internal and external environments, just as our brain waves change according to the state of our consciousness—our thoughts and emotions—as well as our health.

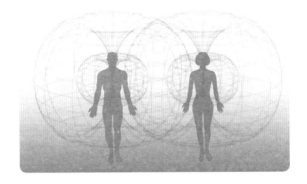

Some Oriental medicine practitioners accept that bioenergy—commonly referred to as *chi, qi,* and *ki*—is a part of the biomagnetic field, or at least very closely associated with it. Pathways along which bioenergy flows in our bodies are called *meridians,* and the openings through which bioenergy enters and leaves are called *meridian points.*

Although attempts are now being made to demonstrate scientifically the existence of meridians and meridian points, it has already been established that the meridian points used in Oriental medicine have higher electrical conductivity than other areas of the skin. In other words, they conduct electricity well.

If you put needles in two meridian points on the same meridian, and then cause a weak electric current to flow between them, you would discover that this pathway is consistent with the flow of the meridian. This means that, as with acupuncture needles or moxibustion, we can use magnetism on meridian points to activate the flow of meridians, and this can affect the biomagnetic field of the human body.

The Earth's Magnetic Field and the Human Magnetic Field Are Closely Connected

All life on Earth has evolved over a long period of time to be optimally adapted to the Earth's magnetic field. All organisms, including individual human beings, have unique biomagnetic fields. As each individual resonates with the magnetic field of the planet, the organism's vital activity is maintained. Consequently, deficiency of or isolation from the Earth's magnetic field would cause abnormalities.

Ecologists in America, seeking to study the effects of the Earth's magnetic field on living organisms, placed mice in a space completely isolated from magnetism. The purpose of this experiment was to identify whether humans can survive in places where gravity does not act at all, as during space travel, and to determine what impact magnetic fields have on the human body.

The study concluded that when in a space without any active magnetic field, mice lose vitality and end up dying because all of their physiological functions decline. In a similar study conducted in Russia in 2008, mice were observed to have suffered a decline in memory and a loss of sociability due to heightened aggressiveness. In addition, the scientists observed changes in internal organs. These studies tell us that severe abnormalities develop in the body once it is outside the influence of the Earth's magnetic field.

According to scientists, the Earth's magnetic field is not always the same, but rather it is continually changing. Moreover, they say that geomagnetic reversals periodically occur; this is a phenomenon in which the Earth's magnetic field reverses its north and south poles as often as every 100,000 years or as seldom as every million years. The movement of the molten iron in the planet's outer core is the main cause of this, and the solar wind is also known to bring changes to the Earth's magnetic field.

Animals with a homing instinct, such as bees, bats, whales, and migratory birds that change their habitat seasonally, have a type of biomagnetism in their brains that acts as a GPS system that detects magnetic fields to find the paths they need to travel. If the planet's magnetic field were to reverse, it would be like searching for a road using a map that had been flipped, with the bottom becoming the top and the top the bottom. This could have fatal implications for these animals.

Geomagnetic reversal, at present, is a natural phenomenon beyond our control. However, scientists are pouring their hearts and souls into related research because this could be a significant change threatening the safety of many organisms.

We are not separate from the Earth. At the level of energy, we and our planet are closely interconnected and influence each other. That's why scholars researching biomagnetic fields even call Mother Earth *Magnetic Mother.*

Everything Is Connected
within Magnetic Fields

If you place a magnet in an empty space, changes develop around it. Although it is invisible, a magnetic field appears. The shape of the field takes on infinite variety according to the shape of the magnet you place there. You can see this easily if you sprinkle iron powder around the magnet.

The effect also differs depending on whether there is one magnet in that space or two. The shape of the energy space also changes depending on whether you place the magnets with the same or different magnetic poles close together. The magnetic fields created by the two magnets affect each other, creating a new energy space.

All vital activity is electromagnetic in character. Therefore, all organisms, including human beings, have their own unique magnetic and energy fields. We can't see them with our eyes, but these connections exist between seemingly separate beings—between humans, between humans and other life-forms, and between humans and the Earth—who, at the level of energy fields, are interconnected and ceaselessly influencing each other.

Recently, honeybees have been dying en masse around the world, shocking many observers. Ninety percent of Korea's native bees have vanished, and the number of domesticated honeybee hives in America has reportedly decreased by one-third over the past several years. This is called *colony collapse disorder*. There are many reasons for this phenomenon, including global warming, the appearance of new viruses, and insecticides. Electromagnetic radiation that results from increased use of cell phones is being considered as another possible explanation. According to proponents of this position, electromagnetic radiation confuses the honeybee's location-tracking ability, so bees go out in search

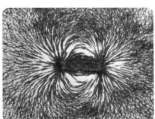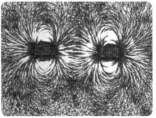

of honey but cannot return to their hive, and they die.

Plants cannot bear fruit if the bees that pollinate them disappear. Such a consequence could impact the global ecosystem, ultimately posing a great threat to human life. This is one example of electromagnetic radiation coming from devices invented by humans threatening the biomagnetic fields of other organisms.

Buddhist thought contains the following story. There is an endlessly wide, infinite, and transparent net, Indra's Net, spread out in the palace of Jeseokchun, one of the many gods of India. Hanging from each knot of this net is a transparent jewel, and these jewels reflect clearly everything in the universe. Each jewel also reflects all the other jewels, so that a wave arising in any one spreads to all the others, and a sound coming from even one reverberates from all the jewels hanging from the net.

The magnetic fields of all things in existence are, in fact, like Indra's Net. Nothing in this world exists in isolation. Everything is interconnected in an unseen energy space.

What Is Magnetic Meditation?

Everything in the world is made up of energy, from a young wildflower growing beside the road to distant stars in the galaxy unseen to the naked eye. I, you, and all human beings are also naturally made up of energy.

Energy cannot be seen or touched, but it can be *felt*. What I intend to convey through Magnetic Meditation is the *feeling* of energy. This is important because if you can feel energy, you can also change it. And with practice, you can control and use that energy beneficially.

Magnetic Meditation is a quick, easy, and effective method of meditation designed to amplify your feeling of energy. As you exert a positive influence on the energy field of your body and mind by using the magnetic fields generated by magnets, you activate your sense for feeling energy. Just as electrical phenomena induce electric current, so, too, you use the power of magnets to induce the flow of bioenergy in your body.

The physical and mental problems we experience are fundamentally rooted in an imbalance of energy.

If you can feel your own energy, then you will become aware of your energy state when it is out of balance, and, furthermore, you will work to recover that balance. If you have no energy sense, or that sense is dull, then you will not be able to readily detect signs of energy imbalance before it manifests as physical and mental problems. Consequently, the sense for feeling and controlling energy should be viewed as a basic necessity and should be acquired by everyone.

Biomagnetic fields exist both inside and outside our bodies. These fields protect us from within and without. Changes great and small, such as in the size, brightness, shape, and vibration of these energy fields, indicate our state of health. Negative changes to energy come when we are tired or sick. The same is true when we suffer emotional confusion or shock. Whether we are angry, sad, despairing, joyful, or excited, all of our energy states affect our energy field. For example, if you've had a big fight with a friend or family member, you have done more than hurt each other emotionally; it's as if you have ripped great holes in each other's energy fields.

Emotion is also energy. Many of the negative emotions we experience develop because the energy system and energy field of our bodies have been disturbed. In contrast with this, changing this energy system and energy field can have a positive effect on our emotions. Energy, which is a subtle current of life, is also a link connecting our bodies and minds. When changes occur in energy, they act like falling dominoes, one change leading to another.

A growing amount of scientific research points to the benefits of meditation in its various forms. Both long-term and short-term effects have been noted. Meditation can relieve stress, improve focus, and restore emotional balance. Some research has even revealed that meditation and other techniques can affect brain fitness at the genetic level. They turn genes on or off, including ones associated with free radicals, inflammation, and cell aging. These techniques have also been shown to alter the body's "fight or flight" response to stressors, making us more resilient to them.

Unfortunately, despite the positive effects of meditation, which are now practically common knowledge, many people still think meditation is difficult. But in fact, meditation is easy. Anyone can do it. The easiest meditation is feeling your energy. I am certain of this, having taught meditation for the last thirty years. To meditate, you have to eliminate distracting thoughts and concentrate. You concentrate naturally in the moment that you feel energy. Magnetic Meditation using a magnet is a method allowing you to feel energy easily and powerfully.

Magnetic Meditation does not necessarily require a lot of time, either. Your energy condition will change a lot if, when you're busy, you do it for just five minutes, two to three times a day. Before a few minutes have passed, your body will grow warmer, saliva will collect in your mouth, and your energy will start to circulate vigorously. You'll feel energy in your hands at first, but, if you continue to concentrate, the feeling will spread to your whole body as the energy is amplified. Generally, a little time is required after you start meditating to allow thoughts to disappear and energy to change in your body. With Magnetic Meditation, though, you can reach such an energy state in just a few minutes.

In the moment, you feel the energy of your body, you communicate with the energy of a greater dimension, and you connect with the great life force of the cosmos. Once that life force enters your body, your imbalanced, disturbed energy field, your ripped, shredded energy field recovers normality and is healed. This is a universal principle of energy that applies to everyone, regardless of race, sex, age, or cultural background.

When your energy changes through Magnetic Meditation, your life will also change. You will get up joyfully in the morning, your voice will grow stronger, your face will shine brighter and more cheerfully, and your steps will fall more lightly. What is more, many positive changes will occur in your different habits, great and small.

The changes we pursue in our lives sometimes begin very small. You are mistaken if you think that meditating for five minutes with a magnet the size of your finger is unlikely to bring amazing changes. Those five minutes are a time when you concentrate completely on yourself. Energy changes through such concentration, and when energy changes, mind and body change. Changes in body and mind spread, ultimately, to change your entire life.

Magnetism Has Long Been Used
for Healing

The main purpose of this book is to enable you to enter a meditative state effectively by developing your energy sense. It is not to introduce Magnetic Therapy, which heals disease using magnetism. However, it would help greatly with your Magnetic Meditation if you learned how magnetism has been used for healing disease in human history and what magnetic principles help heal disease.

People have long thought that it is possible to heal disease and relieve pain by placing a magnet on certain parts of the body. The history of using magnets for healing is very long, especially in Oriental medicine and in Ayurveda, the traditional medicine of India.

In China, magnets were placed on painful areas of the body or turned into powder for use in salves beginning 2,000 years ago. The *Shiji* of Sima Qian recorded that magnets were used to treat the diseases of emperors.

In ancient India, there was a custom of laying out people who were close to death with their heads pointed north. This was because they believed that doing this would align the polarity of the person's body with the polarity of the Earth, alleviating the suffering of death.

Records of healing with magnets are seen in many places in the West, too. The word *magnet* means "stone of magnesia" in Greek. Magnesia was the name of a region of Greece that has a great deal of volcanic rock with magnetic properties. Records indicate that around the third century BCE, magnets were used in Greece as a diarrhea medication, and that around the twelfth century CE, Arab physicians used magnets to treat conditions such as stomach ailments, liver ailments, and baldness.

The ancient Egyptian queen Cleopatra slept with a magnet placed on her forehead and, we are told, enjoyed wearing a necklace made of magnets. This is because she believed that magnets were effective for maintaining youth and beauty. In ancient Rome, magnets were used when treating problems of the eye and colon.

Paracelsus, a famous physician and alchemist from sixteenth-century Sweden, believed in the existence of a life energy that was the basis of the body's natural healing ability. This concept is very similar to that of the *chi*, *qi*, and *ki* spoken of in Oriental medicine. He treated hernia and jaundice using magnets. He believed that magnets invigorated blocked bioenergy and brought balance and harmony to the body.

Franz Anton Mesmer (1734–1815), who can be called

the founder of hypnotic therapy, argued that magnetism was a cure-all and, engaging in somewhat magical medical practices, was criticized by fellow medical scientists at the time. His theories, however, exerted great influence on later generations. He thought that some fluid or force flowing in the bodies of animals was probably related to magnetism, and thus he coined the term *animal magnetism*. Mesmer believed that blockages or interference in the flow of this animal magnetism caused disease.

In modern times, the idea has only been around about sixty years since we started actively using magnetism as an alternative method to treat disease. In the East, many methods have regulated energy and blood circulation by attaching magnets instead of needles to meridians through which ki flows. In the West, many methods have been developed that involve using electric needles or laser needles instead of magnets to stimulate meridian points, as well as exposing part or all of the body to magnetic fields created with electricity.

Magnetic therapy is getting a lot of attention as an alternative therapy because it has no chemical side effects. In Europe, where research in alternative medicine is vigorous, the history of magnetic therapy is a long one. In America, however, it was introduced relatively recently.

Magnetic therapy reportedly has outstanding therapeutic benefits for headache, back/neck/shoulder pain, fatigue, arthritis, depression, high blood pressure, insomnia, fibromyalgia, and multiple sclerosis.

Magnetism Promotes
Blood and Energy Circulation

There is as yet no officially recognized theory demonstrating scientifically why magnetism has a therapeutic effect, and there is little to indicate the nature of its mechanism of action. However, clinical results indicating healing or improvement of specific diseases through the use of magnets or devices that create magnetic fields artificially have been widely reported in the West as well as the East. If we look at this first from the perspective of traditional Oriental medicine, we see that meridians, the paths along which energy flows, are connected to major organs and specific functions of the body. Energy circulates evenly throughout the body and optimum health is maintained when the meridian points are open and energy flows well through the meridians. In contrast with this, if energy is not supplied properly, bodily functions decline, and if serious, disease results. Magnetic therapy facilitates the flow of energy by magnetically stimulating the meridians through which energy flows or by opening the meridian points, through which energy enters and leaves the body.

Magnetic therapy also activates our bodies' blood circulation. In our bodies, about five to six liters of blood flows through the circulatory system. Circulating blood transports oxygen, supplies nutrients, removes waste products generated in the process of metabolism, maintains body temperature, and transports hormones. Accordingly, unless blood circulates well, we easily become tired, do not get an adequate supply of nutrients, and are unable to adequately expel toxins from our bodies.

The blood transports oxygen via the hemoglobin in red blood cells, a protein that contains iron. Because iron is a ferromagnetic substance, placing a magnet close to specific areas of the skin elevates the blood's conductivity, increasing the quantity of ions in the blood. Ionized blood improves blood circulation, stabilizing blood pressure.

Magnetism also reportedly improves the function of the major glands of the endocrine system, including the pineal, pituitary, thyroid, and adrenal glands. Endocrine glands secrete hormones into the bloodstream, playing a very important role, particularly in growth and metabolism. For example, melatonin is a hormone secreted in a concentrated way at night by the pineal gland. This hormone regulates our biorhythms and lets our bodies sleep at night. Symptoms such as depression, insomnia, and decreased libido appear when concentrations of melatonin in the body become imbalanced. Placing a magnet on the forehead is said to be effective for treating insomnia by activating the pineal gland and regulating melatonin secretion.

Magnetic Meditation Balances
the Biomagnetic Field

When we develop health problems, most traditional allopathic treatment focuses on symptoms. However, since symptoms are expressed superficially, eliminating symptoms does not necessarily address the fundamental causes of those problems. Occasionally, treatment of symptoms causes unexpected side effects in other parts of the body. For example, a person who takes a toxic medication to correct problems that developed in his liver might find that, although his liver symptoms have improved, he now has problems in the stomach. For healing beyond the treatment of symptoms, we must go to a deeper level to enable a person to recover the balance of fundamental elements.

There are basic physiological phenomena that change subtly, reflecting the condition of our bodies and minds, including pH balance, biomagnetic field, brain waves, and body temperature. Adjusting the balance of these elements contributes concretely to healing. Balance means a weakly alkaline pH, stable alpha brain waves, a biomagnetic field of an evenly balanced, suitable strength, and body temperatures that are cooler toward the head and warmer toward the lower abdomen.

Magnetic Meditation has great effect on these elements, especially on the biomagnetic field and brain waves. You can maintain the balance of your biomagnetic field by activating your energy sense through Magnetic Meditation. If you focus on the feeling of magnetism and close your eyes at the same time, your brain waves naturally enter an alpha state that relaxes your body and mind.

In my experience, when our brain waves slow below alpha and the biomagnetic fields of our bodies recover appropriate strength and balance, our natural healing abilities are invigorated. Meditation is not based on scientific research. My belief in its effectiveness is based on the anecdotal stories of people who practice it and on my own experience and intuition from having long taught meditation to many people. I earnestly hope that the effects magnetism has on our bodies and minds will be researched in depth and from many angles so that magnetism will be used more broadly in healing and meditation.

The Heart of Magnetic Meditation Is
Recovering the Zero Point

What, then, must we do to escape from emotions, habits, and desires to recover a zero-point state of consciousness? It is like finding that center point on my floating globe.

To get the globe to float above its stand, first you have to take the globe from the stand. In the same way, to escape from negative patterns of emotion, habit, and desire, first you must separate the pattern from yourself, so you can look at it objectively. Meditation is this process of objectifying and observing yourself. The heart of Magnetic Meditation is developing a sense for objectifying and watching yourself through energy sensations—in other words, a sense for restoring your zero point.

The simple act of floating a globe in the air is not as easy as it looks. It requires practice. How much more unlikely is it, then, that we recover our zero point—that is, harmony and balance—across the whole of our lives in a moment? Fortunately, within us naturally is a sense for achieving balance with other people, other organisms, and all beings, as well as for recovering balance in our own bodies and minds. Many of the personal and social problems we face develop from our loss of this sense for natural harmony and balance. We must now awaken and restore that sense.

People naturally want to get closer to what they like and move farther away from what they dislike. There is a trap here, though. Good things are not always good; bad things are not always bad. So don't become too caught up in what you like. Fighting never ends when you are bound to rigid conceptions of "good" and "bad." Moreover, there is no guarantee that what you like will last forever. Being "good" is a relative value that changes constantly with the times and conditions.

If so far you have been pursuing only what you like, try to seek what is truly important to you instead. By "important," I mean that which comes from the center of your consciousness. What you like, on the other hand, is based solely on what is comfortable to deal with. For example, you may not be attracted to environmental and social issues like water and air quality, the Earth, peace, and conscience. But nevertheless, these things are indispensable for your survival, and thus are unmistakably important. Your energy becomes properly centered when you have absolute values of this sort instead of relative values, when you focus on important things instead of only on things you like.

Our emotions rise and fall ceaselessly like waves, according to our likes and dislikes. When what's important—absolute values—is at the center of our lives, we can look with disinterest at the waves of emotions that rise and fall within the strong magnetic field of life. Once this happens, we are no longer easily swept up by emotion, and even if we are swept up in emotion, we can recover our lost balance in no time. We are able to change and create energy autonomously, living our lives in observer consciousness with a restored zero point that leans toward no polarity, positive or negative.

Basics

CHAPTER

2

Before Beginning Magnetic Meditation

Magnetic Meditation uses magnets to activate our senses for feeling our bodies' energy and energy fields. We concentrate and meditate automatically while we are feeling energy. Stress relief, improved concentration, and revitalization come naturally in this process.

The magnets are carriers of the flow of life, and that flow creates energy fields that are unique for each person. If you use a magnet, you can feel this energy field a little more quickly, easily, and effectively. If you bring a magnet close to your body, you are likely to experience a variety of feelings. These sensations may include the sense of a pushing and pulling force or a tingling sensation like a mild electric current. You may also feel heat and a sense of heavy resistance, as you may feel when you move your hand slowly in water. These feelings come not only from the magnetic field of the magnet itself, but also from the biomagnetic fields of our bodies, which are activated and amplified by the magnet.

When doing Magnetic Meditation, it's important to focus on the energy sensations of our bodies, rather than on the magnets themselves. Instead of using specific movements or training methods, while you're moving, concentrate on the energy created by that movement and the energy space. Through this, your concentration will develop, you will be able to meditate more easily, and you will develop a different perspective of yourself, allowing you to objectively observe yourself and your situation.

Two Energy Principles to Remember

I want you to remember two important energy principles when you do Magnetic Meditation.

First, remember that energy goes where your mind goes. In other words, energy goes wherever you focus, and where energy goes, physical changes occur. This principle is similar to the *observer effect* spoken of in particle physics. Continue to break down all matter in the universe, and you find that, ultimately, you reach small particles that cannot be divided any further. These particles reportedly move in directions the observer expects them to move. If you focus your mind on a desired part of your body, energy will go there, and changes will take place as a result. Remember that the unseen mind, the world of consciousness, creates visible phenomena.

Second, all things are interconnected through energy. We include two-person training methods and healing in Magnetic Meditation because energy sensitivity greatly increases when two people do it together, but also, and more importantly, because two people can feel with their bodies that all things are interconnected through energy. If you experience through feeling that you and the other person are connected as one through an energy field, your attitude toward the other person and toward living things around you will change in a positive direction.

Once you have sufficiently practiced feeling energy using a magnet, try doing it without one. Those who have had trouble feeling energy will feel energy much more easily, and those who have had good energy sensitivity will experience that sense much more finely and strongly.

Energy is the flow of life, so sensing energy is sensing life. Once people regain this sense, they recover once-lost balance, harmony, and vitality. When the frozen ground melts and the land fills with life in the spring, water rises in the trees, their leaves open, and their flowers bloom. In the same way, when energy fills our bodies, physical health and emotional abundance come automatically.

Precautions for Magnetic Meditation

The main purpose of Magnetic Meditation is not using magnets to heal disease. Moreover, the magnets included with this book are not a medical product. Although magnets reportedly have no significant side effects, persons with serious ailments should consult with a medical professional before using them. The following are general precautions to keep in mind when doing Magnetic Meditation.

- If you have an artificial implant, such as a cardiac pacemaker, you should not use magnets. Their magnetic fields could affect and damage such devices.
- If you wear a hearing aid, use the magnets with your hearing aid removed. Store the magnets somewhere away from your hearing aid.
- Do not use the magnets if you have a metal medical prosthesis in your body.

- Pregnant women should not use the magnets. Their magnetic fields could affect the fetus, whose energy is still weak.
- Do not use the magnets on injuries that are bleeding or that have not yet healed. Although opinions on this differ, exercise caution since some believe that bleeding could be aggravated by magnetism.
- Do not use the magnets continuously for a long time. Take particular care not to fall asleep with a magnet placed on your body.
- Some people may experience slight dizziness after using a magnet. If you shake out your arms and legs or do light stretching when this happens, you will recover right away.
- You should wait at least one hour after eating before using magnets.
- After using the magnets, in a standing position, gently shake out your arms and legs, and sweep your hands over your whole body. Doing some light stretching is good, too.
- You should keep the magnets out of the reach of children under eight.
- Magnets can cause problems in videotapes, CDs, computers, televisions and other electronic devices and credit cards, so keep them at least four inches from such items.

Playing with and Getting
to Know Your Magnets

You probably remember playing with magnets when you were little. You were probably amazed by how you could use a horseshoe magnet or bar magnet to pick up a bunch of paperclips or nails all sticking to each other. Or, you wondered how the magnet would draw magnetic lines when you sprinkled iron powder around it. Let's take some time to return to the curiosity of our childhood, playing and becoming familiar with magnets and their magnetic fields.

Use your fingers to hold the magnets vertically in your hands, and then repeatedly bring them closer together and farther apart. Feel them pulling or pushing against each other. The north and south poles of the Energy Magnets enclosed in this book are on the left and right of the magnet body—not at the tips. Magnetism is strongest at the thickest part of the magnet body. You can also feel both polarities at the pointed ends, unlike with a bar magnet, because of its almond shape. If you rotate the body of a magnet a little, you'll feel the direction of the force change accordingly. As you slowly move them, try to focus on the feelings you get between the magnets, as well as around the magnets and your hands.

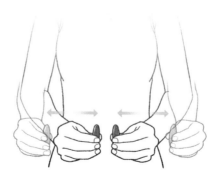

Use your fingers to hold the magnets sideways in your hands, and move your hands in circles, rotating them as if pedaling a bicycle. Try changing the direction of your circles, too. Do rotations with the ends of the magnets facing each other, and also with the ends pointed up and down. Also try moving them in very small and very large circles. See how the feeling changes whenever you change your movement.

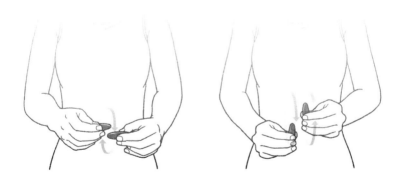

Place one magnet above a finger, and the other below it. The two magnets are stuck to your finger by magnetism. Carefully move your hand around a little. Notice the two magnets stay in position. It's the same principle as was involved in the games we used to play when we were little: for instance, placing a paperclip on a piece of paper and moving a magnet around below it, watching the clip move along with the magnet. Magnetism, the power of the magnet, is transmitted even through your flesh and bone.

Turning a Screw

Put two magnets together, and then rapidly rotate one as if you were turning a screw. One magnet whirls, spinning while remaining stuck to the other one. Try turning the opposite magnet in the same way. After sticking three magnets together, try using the same method to turn one or both of the outside magnets.

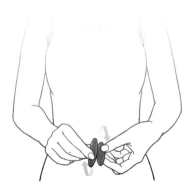

Place one magnet on a flat surface, and then hold another in your hand so that about half of its pointed end is visible. Make circles with the hand holding the magnet about one to two inches above the magnet you placed on the table. Magnetism will cause the bottom magnet to rotate along with it. Adjusting the distance between the two magnets and the speed with which you make circles, try to get the magnet on the table spinning rapidly like a top. Also try doing it holding two magnets.

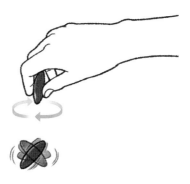

Place two or three magnets on a desk with about two to three inches between them. Spin one of the magnets with your hand. As the magnet moves, spinning, the other magnets will also spin, and soon they'll clatter together and stick. Sometimes, the other magnets will jump into the air, as if performing a noisy acrobatic trick. Also try this using more magnets. If you rotate one magnet, the others will move along with it, until they come together with a clacking sound, sticking to form a kebab.

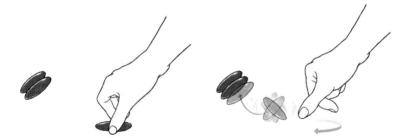

Hold a magnet vertically in one hand on a desk, so that its ends point up and down. With the other hand, hold another magnet in the same way, and bring it close—but not enough to stick—to the first magnet, positioning it above the one you're holding on the desk. Carefully open your bottom hand, letting go of the magnet, and lower your upper hand until the two magnets stick together, creating what looks like two sausages.

Use the same method you did in Making Sausages, but, this time, try to get the bottom magnet to stand up while maintaining a small space between the two magnets, without letting them touch. With a little practice, anyone can develop a feeling for this balance. Try to maintain this state as long as possible.

Holding out your palm in front of you, place two magnets on your fingers about one inch apart and hold them in place with your thumb. From this position, toss the two magnets simultaneously into the air. As they spin in the air, the magnets will stick together with a clacking sound. The higher you toss the magnets, the longer you can make the sound last.

Feeling an Energy Field with Magnets

Now, while using the Energy Magnets, take some time to feel your body's energy field, the space inhabited by your body's energy. To amplify that feeling, use whichever hand is most energy sensitive to feel the energy coming from the magnets, and then move your hand to feel energy in other parts of your body.

You should do this exercise in a quiet location that's good for concentration, rather than somewhere noisy and crowded with people. Closing your eyes really helps when you have trouble concentrating. You can then feel the subtle energy sensations in your body much more clearly because you have shut out visual stimulation.

Hold a magnet vertically in each hand with your fingers. First, spin the magnets a little, adjusting them so that they pull on each other. In this state, close your eyes and slowly bring the two magnets together just enough so that they don't stick to each other. Then pull them apart to about the width of your trunk and repeat these movements. When the magnets pull on each other, the energy in your body gathers, closing toward its center.

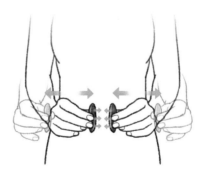

Now rotate the bodies of the magnets slightly, adjusting them so that they push against each other. In this state, close your eyes and repeatedly move the two magnets closer together and then farther apart. When the magnets repel each other, the energy in your body expands, spreading outward.

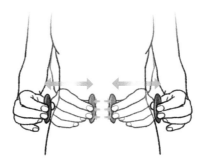

Use your fingers to hold the magnets sideways in your hands, and move your hands in small circles, rotating them as if pedaling a bicycle. Try to turn your attention to the irregular, uneven feeling of energy pushing and pulling. The magnets will probably squirm in your hands, and you'll even get a tingling sensation in your palms and fingers. Sensitive people can detect these feelings spreading along their wrists and arms to their whole body. If you repeatedly induce this pulling and pushing force as you rotate the magnets, the energy in your body will be activated and amplified as it repeatedly contracts and relaxes, opens and closes. If you continue these movements, your mind will settle down and grow calmer, and your breathing will become more comfortable. This exercise is also great for developing focus.

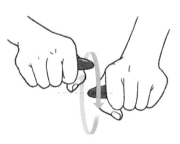

This time, open the palm of one hand, and with the other hand hold a magnet so that its tip points downward. Bring the hand holding the magnet over your open palm, and use it to make small circles about one inch above the center of your palm. Stop making circles, and repeatedly bring the magnet close to your palm and then move it farther away. As the center of your palm tingles, you can sense the feeling spreading along your wrists and arms to other parts of your body. You may even feel the energy field surrounding your hand like a cloud, or you may sense what feels like a very thick glove of energy on your hand.

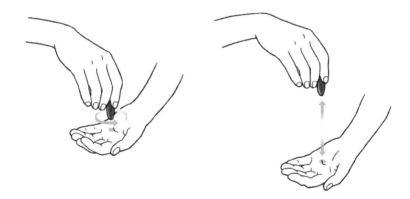

Place a magnet in the palm of each hand, hold one hand above the other, and then concentrate on the feelings in your palms quietly for one minute. There will be a stinging, tingling sensation, as if electric current were flowing between the palms of your hands. Now hold your bottom hand in place in front of your lower abdomen, and slowly raise your upper hand to the height of your chest, then lower it again, repeating this motion. Focus your attention on how the feeling changes when the gap between your hands increases and decreases. You will feel intense magnetism between the palm of one hand and the back of the other. In particular, the very middle of your palms will be activated.

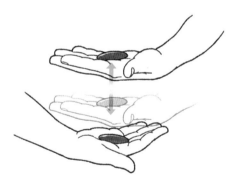

Just as the magnetism grows greater when you stick many magnets together, so, too, you can feel the energy field growing greater when many people get together to experience energy. Now, with friends and family, let's try to feel energy using magnets.

Two people sit facing each other. One person turns her palms upward and places magnets lengthwise on her fingers. The other person gently grasps magnets by the middle, holding them in her hands. Then, holding them above the other person's magnets, she repeatedly moves them closer to and then farther away from the other person's magnets. To keep the magnets below from continually rising to meet the ones above, the person whose hands are below should gently hold them in place between her middle and ring fingers. Also try switching roles, and then talk about what you feel.

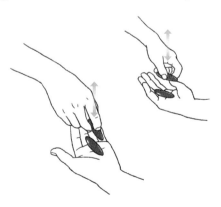

This time, one person holds her magnets in her fists so that the tip of each magnet is visible above them. The other person holds her magnets in her fists so that the tip of each magnet is visible below them, and then she slowly moves her fists in circles above the first person's hands so that the magnets protruding below her fists circle those sticking out above her partner's fists, as if she were grinding grain with a grindstone. You'll feel whirling tunnels of energy or feel as if there are unseen bumps in space. Also try switching roles, and then talk about what you feel.

When several people do this exercise together, they should all hold their left palm up and place a magnet on it, and their right palm down, closed around a magnet. In this position, they should hold their left hand below the right hand of the person to their left and their right hand above the left hand of the person to their right. Keeping their left hands still, everyone should repeatedly move only their right hand up and down, so that their magnet moves closer and farther away from the left hand of the person beside them. You will likely sense a tingling feeling of electric current, as if a power line connects your hands with those of the people next to you.

This time, wrap your left hand around a magnet so that its pointed end extends above your left fist, and wrap your right hand around a magnet so that its pointed end extends below your right fist. In this position, hold your left hand below the right hand of the person to your left and your right hand above the left hand of the person to your right. Now, keeping your left hand still, circle only your right hand as if grinding grain with a grindstone, slowly moving it around in circles above the magnet of the person to your right. Although you're moving only your right hand while keeping your left hand still, you can sense the feeling of magnetism being amplified in both hands.

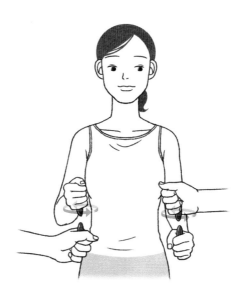

One person closes his eyes, holding both hands out, palms open, facing up. The other person uses a magnet to make small circles about one inch above the middle of one of his partner's palms. He then repeatedly brings the magnet close to the middle of his partner's palm, and then he moves it away. The partner who has his eyes closed tries to guess which side the magnet is on. He tries to guess whether the magnet is making a circle or being moved up and down. The partners also try switching roles. At first, you will feel an intense magnetism in the palm where the magnet is close, and soon you will sense the feeling spreading to your other hand, as well.

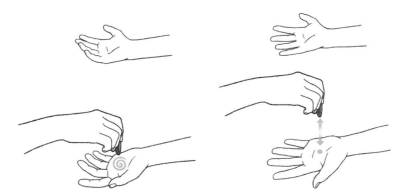

Strengthening an Energy Field
with Magnets

As you accumulate stress or fatigue, you are bound to experience a change of energy. People commonly say, "I have no energy," when they don't want to do anything because they feel physically and mentally drained. If you don't move your body at all when you feel this way, your energy stagnates, and your body grows heavier, like a soggy cotton ball. When this happens, try strengthening your body's energy field simply and quickly using magnets.

Although they're not visible to our eyes, there are paths in our bodies along which energy travels. These are called meridians in Oriental medicine, and the channels through which energy enters and exits our bodies are called meridian points. There are similar concepts in yoga, too. Places where energy gathers powerfully in our bodies are called *chakras*. *Chakra* is Sanskrit for "wheel." Our bodies typically have seven chakras. Although invisible anatomically, chakras—which, in concept, are like the body's energy power plants—can be felt by anyone once his or her energy sensitivity has developed. The locations of the seven chakras are near the genitals, the lower abdomen, the solar plexus, the chest, the throat, the forehead, and the crown of the head.

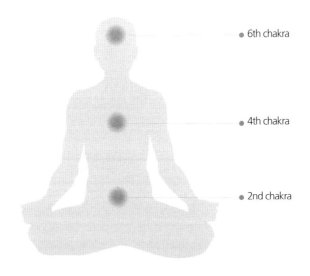

6th chakra

4th chakra

2nd chakra

Using a magnet, it's possible to stimulate the first through the seventh chakras in sequence. You can also get significant benefit just by stimulating the three main energy centers located in the belly, the chest, and the forehead.

Of these, the second chakra—located about two inches down from the belly button and another two inches into the abdomen—is responsible for our bodies' physical activity. The second chakra stores energy and circulates it to the whole body. The body achieves energetic balance when the second chakra is strengthened, helping to maintain the body in an optimum state of health and assisting its natural healing ability. The second chakra also stabilizes a person psychologically, resulting in better concentration and perseverance, powerful drive, and overflowing confidence.

Located in the center of the chest, the fourth chakra manages the energy of emotion. Development of the fourth chakra leads a person to feel peace and calm and to experience a welling up of love in the heart. If the fourth chakra is blocked due to stress or negative emotions, the nervous and circulatory systems will suffer. If this sort of blockage persists, a person may develop various psychological illnesses.

Located in the "third eye" slightly above the center point between the eyebrows, the sixth chakra is closely related to the brain. Rational judgment becomes precise and concentration improves when the sixth chakra is activated. A variety of mental powers develop, including the ability to get to the heart of a problem, to come up with new ideas for solving difficult issues, and to create new things by interconnecting diverse elements or areas that outwardly seem unrelated.

These three energy centers, although they have different energies, make up a single, highly cooperative system within our bodies. Developing these three chakras results in physical health, emotional abundance, and heightened mental ability, which will bring balance to life.

The basics of Magnetic Meditation include using magnets to activate the senses of the hands, strengthening the energy centers in the belly, chest, and forehead, and then meditating so that these three energy centers are linked as one. Since you have already activated the energy senses in your hands using magnets, now strengthen the three places in your body with the most important energy fields.

Hold one magnet sideways in the fingers of each hand with the tips of the two magnets facing each other about one to two inches from your belly and use them to make little circles. Keep your lower back comfortably straight, bend your head forward slightly, and close your eyes so that you barely see out of them. Be careful not to bend your neck too far forward, looking down at your lower abdomen, as this hinders energy circulation. As you repeat this for three to five minutes, try to notice any sensations in your lower abdomen.

While you circle the magnets, open your mouth slightly and exhale deeply. A warm feeling of heat will develop in your belly, and if you concentrate, that feeling of heat will grow more powerful, spreading to your hips, the circumference of your waist, and even your lower back. Your breathing automatically grows deeper, saliva pools in your mouth, and power fills your lower abdomen. If you continue to concentrate, you will feel a sense of space in your belly, and you will get the feeling that this space is growing deeper and wider. While concentrating, continue to develop that sensation.

Use your thumbs to hold one or two magnets in each of your hands and bring them in front of your abdomen. Ensure that you have about three to four inches of space between your belly and hands. In this position, cup the palms of your hands, and, for about one minute, quietly charge your lower abdomen with energy while imagining a beam of sunlight shining on it from the palms of your hands. This time, for one minute, repeatedly push your hands forward when you inhale and pull them toward your belly when you exhale. Doing this, even for a short time, allows the heat that has gathered in your head to sink into your belly as your whole body grows lighter.

Hold one magnet in the fingers of each hand with the tips of the two magnets facing each other about one to two inches from your chest and use them to make little circles. The direction you draw the circles doesn't matter, so just circle the magnet tips in whichever direction is comfortable for you. Straighten your lower back, bend your neck very slightly, and close your eyes. Continue to circle the magnets for three to five minutes as you concentrate on your chest. With your body growing warmer, your chest will automatically feel more comfortable. You'll get the feeling that your heart is opening up, like the aperture of a camera opening or like something melting or dye spreading in water. The energy spreads through your body as this happens. While you circle the magnets, open your mouth slightly and exhale deeply.

Hold one magnet in the fingers of each hand and bring your hands to your third eye, which is located on your forehead between your eyebrows. Use the magnets to make little circles, their tips facing each other about one to two inches from your forehead. Notice the sensations of energy as you continue this for three to five minutes. You'll likely experience a feeling of magnetism pulling and pushing between the magnets and your forehead, and you may feel a tingling or crawling sensation in or around your head. If you continue to concentrate, your head will become clearer and cooler as you sense a kind of heavy heat leaving it. You may even feel an energy field surrounding your head like a capsule. While you circle the magnets, open your mouth slightly and exhale deeply.

Let's try unifying the energy fields of our belly, chest, and brain, which are our bodies' most important energy centers. Open one hand, palm up, in front of your lower abdomen and place a magnet in it. Use the thumb of your other hand to hold a magnet and turn it downward to face your other palm with space between your hands. Keeping one hand in front of your lower abdomen, breathe in, slowly pulling your other hand up to the top of your head. Breathe out again, and very slowly lower the hand you had raised, as if brushing your body, bringing it close to your other hand so that the two magnets you hold almost—but not quite— touch. Repeat this movement several times.

Most importantly, focus on the feelings you experience between your head, chest, and lower abdomen. You will feel as though a heavy pillar of energy is sinking and rising between your head and lower abdomen with the movement of your hand, and you'll sense the energy fields of the three points in your body connecting. When the major energy centers of your body are all activated, your lower abdomen will grow warmer, your chest more comfortable, and your head cooler. When you are in such an energy state, your body becomes healthier, you focus automatically, and creative ideas come to mind easily.

Everyone has their own energy field. Although this biomagnetic field is not ordinarily visible, people with very acute energy senses concretely perceive the biomagnetic fields in themselves and others. If this biomagnetic field grows weak, a person is readily stressed or easily fatigued. She is also easily influenced by the negative energies of her environment or the people around her. Let's create vibrant health by using a magnet to strengthen the whole body's biomagnetic field in a short time.

With one hand, hold a magnet so that the point faces your body. Close your eyes to help you concentrate. As if wrapping your body in an energy coil, move the magnet in coiling lines from the top of your head to the tips of your toes, creating an energy field. Do this slowly and with devotion, as though you're giving the most beautiful and precious gift in the world to the person you love and care about the most.

Next, beginning in the center of your forehead, move the magnet past your face toward the outside of your head, creating an energy field by slowly drawing a vortex. It doesn't matter whether the vortex you're drawing turns in a clockwise or counterclockwise direction. Just do it whichever way is comfortable to you. Next, beginning in the middle of your chest and going toward the outside of your trunk, use the same method to draw a vortex, expanding your energy field. Lastly, beginning at your lower abdomen and moving toward your lower back, hips, and legs, use the same method to draw a vortex, strengthening your energy field.

Finally, use the magnet to draw a large circle surrounding your whole body. Imagine yourself sitting inside a massive, circular energy field. Repeat this several times until you get the feeling that your body is surrounded by a powerful energy field.

Meditation for Attracting What You Want

After doing Magnetic Body training for strengthening your whole body's energy field, sit comfortably with one magnet in each hand and place your hands on your knees. It's fine to sit on the floor or in a chair. If you sit on the floor, you don't necessarily have to sit in a half-lotus posture. It's okay to sit comfortably with your legs crossed. If sitting is uncomfortable, then lie down on the floor. It doesn't matter.

Close your eyes and try to feel the powerful energy field surrounding your body. Imagine that your whole body has become a powerful magnet through magnetism. Imagine that your energy field, all the energy fields around you, and the energy field of the whole Earth are resonating in unison in perfect rhythm.

In that state, bring to mind what you want. Imagine that it is being powerfully attracted to the area around your body, which is now a magnet. Health, happiness, economic abundance, good personal relationships, changes of habit—it doesn't matter what it is. Imagine that everything you want—whether some object, person, a certain emotion, or an energy state—is moving toward you because you have become an energy magnet.

Fill yourself up with joy and satisfaction as you imagine that what you want has already been realized. And have a heart of genuine gratitude for all the people and conditions that have helped to make this come true. Give thanks for the great life force of the cosmos that has always permitted you infinite potential and the best of things, even if you were unaware of it.

Energy Meditation without a Magnet

If you've had plenty of practice using a magnet to feel energy and expand your energy field, then now it's time to attempt this without a magnet. The energy you feel using only the senses of your body is much softer and deeper than when you use a magnet. If you have trouble feeling the energy, repeat the "Feeling an Energy Field with Magnets" exercise (page 58) several times, and then immediately imitate that feeling using only your hands without a magnet.

Once you are sure that you feel an energy field between your hands, you can experience all of the Magnetic Meditation introduced in this book without magnets, using only your body's senses. Basically, all you have to do is apply the energy sense of your hands instead of relying on magnets. This is true of all the training methods included in the Applications section of this book, as well as the meditation methods in the Basics section. The more you use your energy sense, the more subtle and powerful it will grow. You should try to practice whenever you have the time, and take time to commune and communicate through energy with your family and friends.

The principles of energy are universal, applicable to everything in the world, not only our bodies. Once your sense for feeling and applying energy develops, it begins to exert a positive effect on all domains of your life, including your health, family, work, and personal relationships.

Sit in a chair or on the floor with your lower back comfortably straight. Place your hands on your knees and relax your shoulders, chest, and arms. Slowly inhale and exhale. Repeat this several times until you feel comfortable. With your palms facing upward, slowly lift your hands off your knees, raising them to waist height. Concentrate your awareness on your hands. As you focus on the feelings in your palms, slowly raise your hands to chest height, and then lower them again to waist height. Slowly continue to repeat this movement. Over time, you will develop a weighty feeling in your palms and will feel as if an unseen pillar of energy has appeared above them.

Slowly bring your hands to the height of your chest. Turn your palms to face each other, leaving a little space between them. Concentrate your awareness on the space between your palms. Slowly move your hands apart so that there is about five to six inches between your palms. Move your hands apart slowly as if they are pushing against each other.

Now reduce the space between your hands to about one to two inches. Keep your palms from touching each other. Continue slowly repeating the motion of expanding and contracting the space between your hands. Keep focusing your awareness on your hands as you imagine the energy between your palms being gradually amplified.

If you are getting even a very subtle feeling in your hands, focus on that feeling. You might feel a sense of heat or a tingling sense of electricity. You could get a feeling of magnetism and volume, as if there were a balloon between the palms of your hands. You will feel the energy field between your hands expanding and contracting, as when you used a magnet. Gently push your hands closer together and pull them farther apart, like a butterfly slowly flapping its wings. Keep repeating these motions as you develop the feeling of magnetism between your hands.

When you use the pushing and pulling of a magnet to feel energy and then feel the energy only through your body's senses without a magnet, you'll realize a very important fact. You can change the pushing force and pulling force you feel between your hands simply by changing your thought and intention. This means that you can change the polarity of energy with the power of thought, or, to put it another way, you can cause instant changes in objective, physical states through thought.

When feeling energy without a magnet, if you think about energy pushing outward between your hands, a pushing force will actually develop between them, gradually moving your hands apart. Conversely, thinking that energy between your hands is pulling on them creates a pulling force, and your hands are brought closer together by this force. Your thoughts and intentions become commands, and the energy between your hands accordingly creates pulling and pushing forces.

The ability to intentionally control and change the polarity of energy is a tremendous discovery. It is ultimately the secret of all creation. All creation begins with a thought—that is, with an intention. Experiencing your own thoughts manifesting as changes of energy and practicing this repeatedly expands that experience to your entire life. The experience of changing energy through your thoughts and intentions will bring many positive changes to your life. You will gain confidence and creativity, and you will be able to improve your lifestyle habits—like eating fresh vegetables instead of fast food, changing your career, or achieving some great goal you have been dreaming of your whole life.

Applications

Meditation for Increasing Concentration

Whether you focus on work, studies, or hobbies, it is difficult to obtain the best results without immersion and concentration. Concentration requires focusing your attention completely on the present moment without being hindered by distracting thoughts. There are two meditation methods for increasing concentration that are effective and can be easily practiced by anyone. One is focusing on *energy*, the other, focusing on *breath*. All the methods included in the Basics section brought the effects of meditation naturally through concentration on energy sensations. You can greatly improve your concentration and further deepen your meditative practice by adding breath to these techniques.

Before entering meditation, it's important to first open blockages in your body to facilitate energy circulation. Relaxing the area of the head, face, neck, and shoulders, in particular, greatly helps enhance concentration because it improves the flow of blood and energy going to the brain.

Meditate somewhere free from noise and the interference of other people. You can do this meditation sitting on the floor or in a chair. Although it's okay to do it with your eyes open, it's much more effective if you close your eyes. First, do in sequence the methods introduced in steps one through five below, becoming comfortable with all the steps. Later, you can choose only the steps you want to do, those that fit your situation or energy state. You can get a satisfactory effect by only doing steps four and five if your body has been made sufficiently ready by other preparatory exercises. Although it's all right for beginners to turn on some light meditation music, it's better to do the exercises without music once you are comfortable with them.

Hold a magnet with your fingers and gently tap your entire head with it. Tap the top, front, sides, and back of your head, the back of your neck, and your shoulders without missing a spot. Be careful not to tap so hard that it hurts. While you're tapping, open your mouth slightly and exhale slowly. Although this exercise looks so simple, you will be surprised by its effects when you actually do it. Your head will feel refreshed in no time.

Step 2: Stimulating the Energy Points of the Head

Hold a magnet with your fingers and make small circles with it along the boundary where the skin of your face meets your hair, gently massaging this area. Beginning at the top and middle of your forehead, massage the entire area evenly, all the way to the area around your ears and the base of your skull at the back of your neck. Next, massage the major energy points of the head and face as indicated in the graphic on page 131. While you're massaging, open your mouth gently and exhale slowly.

Hold a magnet in one hand so that its end is pointed toward your face. Sweep away stagnant, heavy energy from
the center toward the outside of your face and head as
if you were sweeping your face with a soft brush. As you
sweep, hold the magnet at a slight distance so that it
does not directly touch your skin. Open your mouth
gently and exhale as slowly as possible. Imagine that the
stagnant energies that have built up around your head
and face are all being purified and leaving your body
with your exhaled breath.

Now create an energy field around your face and head using the magnet. Keeping about two to three inches between your hand and face, use the magnet to draw a winding line as if wrapping an energy coil from the crown of your head to your neck, covering it with the curtain made of a magnetic field. Next, still holding the magnet in your hand, create a magnetic field curtain from your forehead to the back of your head, as if brushing back your hair. This time, move your hand freely, wrapping the curtain of a magnetic field around your entire face and head and strengthening your energy field.

Situated between and slightly above the eyebrows, the third eye has been known since ancient times as an important energy point for increasing concentration and bringing insight. This point is even depicted as a jewel on the forehead of the Buddha on Buddhist statues and paintings. There are generally three methods for stimulating the third eye with a magnet: directly touching the third eye with a magnet, holding a magnet at a distance of about one inch from the third eye, and making small circles with a magnet at a distance of about one inch from the third eye. Choose any one of these or use all three methods sequentially. Stimulate your third eye for about one to two minutes using the method most suitable to you. You will soon feel your third eye and the area around it opening and closing like a camera aperture. It will be a pulsing, tingling, or crawling feeling.

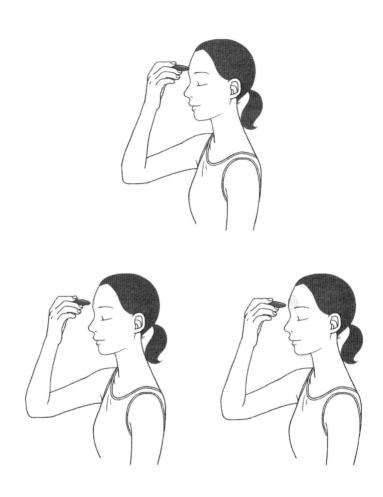

Once you sense that your third eye has been activated to a certain degree, hold the magnets vertically using your thumbs and other fingers as shown in the picture and bring them slowly in front of your forehead. Bring the magnets to about one inch of each other, and then pull them away so that they just go past the sides of your head. Repeat this while concentrating on your third eye. This exercise is much more effective if you imagine your brain repeatedly expanding and contracting as if it were breathing, timed to the movement of your hands.

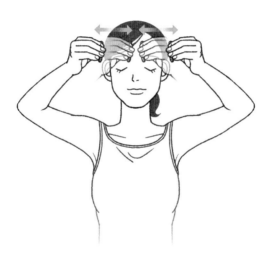

Step 5: Meditating with Breath

While holding the magnets, rest your hands on your knees. Open your hands comfortably, palms up, and let the magnets sit in the centers of your palms. Straighten your lower back, inhale deeply, and exhale. Just let yourself breathe without trying to control your respiration. Count each time you inhale and exhale as one breath, starting at one and continuing until you reach five. Once you count to five, start over with one.

If counting to five is easy, then try counting to ten using the same method. Although it doesn't seem demanding, an unexpectedly large number of people forget what number they're on before they count to ten because of their distracting thoughts. So there is no need to become discouraged or blame yourself just because you forget what number you're on.

If you miss your count because random thoughts distracted you, just begin counting again from one. The more you try to suppress these thoughts, the more they snowball out of control. To overcome this, you have to let go of those thoughts, not fight with them. When distracting thoughts come to you, just let them be, without trying to shake them off. Accept the fact that distracting thoughts have come to mind and just concentrate again on your breathing.

Continue to focus on the feeling of your breath coming in and going out. Imagine life energy entering your body with your breath, supplying your body and brain with fresh oxygen and energy. When you exhale, imagine the stagnant energy that has accumulated in your body leaving with your breath.

Meditating by focusing on your breath in this way for ten minutes a day will enhance your concentration to an amazing degree. Doing it for even three minutes can be effective when you're busy.

Meditation for Eliminating Stress

If you find yourself irritated over trivial things, showing anger to those around you without really knowing why, or sighing often, stop what you're doing and take just twenty minutes of your time for Magnetic Meditation. Continuing to work when you're in stress up to your neck is just like running with a bomb in your hands.

Stress is one of our bodies' important survival systems, one we cannot and must not do without. It's like food. We can't survive without eating food, but over-eating causes indigestion. Appropriate stress increases motivation, spurring us on toward self-development and growth. Excessive stress, however, and especially chronic stress that we build up without timely release, is a major culprit ruining the health of our bodies and minds.

Magnetic Meditation for Eliminating Stress is designed to open blockages in the energy center of your chest as it releases stagnant, frustrated energy. It then fills up your chest with bright, fresh energy. You can do it sitting on the floor or in a chair, or you can do it lying down. When you do it lying down, spread your arms to about fifteen degrees from your trunk. It's good to have your palms facing upward and your legs spread naturally.

Chest Tapping

If you have a lot of stress, unpurified emotional energy accumulates in your chest. This is also why you end up pounding your chest with your fists without even realizing it when you are angry or frustrated. Feelings of frustration will recede a great deal, and you will feel much lighter if you just gently tap the area of your chest. Hold a magnet with your fingers and gently and evenly tap below your shoulder blades, above your chest, on the indentation in the middle of your chest, under the ribs below your chest, and along your sides. Be careful not to tap so hard that it hurts. While you're tapping, gently open your mouth and exhale slowly.

Using the end of a magnet, gently press the places you were tapping before, kneading and massaging evenly as you move in circles. Also, as shown in the following picture, massage the energy points located between your chest and shoulders using the same method. Do the same on the energy point situated in the concave part of the middle of your chest. Massage it until it feels refreshed. This major energy point is often blocked by accumulated stress. When this point is blocked, you readily feel discomfort in your belly and tightness in your chest. Imagine that the frustration, anger, worries, and anxieties lumped together in your chest are leaving your body as you exhale.

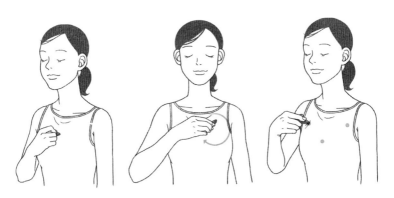

Hold the magnet with your fingers and use it to brush away the stagnant energy from the center of your chest downward along your trunk and both arms. Keep some distance between the magnet and your body so that it doesn't touch your skin directly. Next, gently touch the center of your chest with the end of the magnet and hold it there for about one minute. Your breathing will automatically grow deeper, and, as this happens, you'll feel cool energy entering your body from the center of your chest. Next, use the magnet to make little circles, holding it about one inch from your chest. Then you'll get the feeling that your chest is opening like a camera aperture, and that feeling will spread to your whole body.

Repeat this movement for about two to three minutes. When you get the feeling that your chest area has been activated, draw a vortex from the center of your chest outward, strengthening the energy fields of your chest and whole body. Before you realize it, you'll experience your chest growing cooler, a feeling of blockages opening, and, sometimes, a feeling that blockages are melting down.

Slowly lower onto your knee the hand holding the magnet. If you're doing this exercise lying down, lower your hand onto the floor. Open your hand naturally, palm up, and be sure a magnet is placed in the center of your palm. Inhale and exhale comfortably without trying to control your breathing.

When you inhale, be conscious of the energy point at the center of your chest, and when you exhale, imagine that the stagnant energy in your chest is leaving through your fingertips as you focus your attention on your chest, shoulders, elbows, wrists, and fingertips, in that order. Gently open your mouth and exhale slowly. If it's hard to imagine energy leaving your body from your chest all the way out to your fingertips, then, with your eyes open, hold a magnet in one hand slightly away from your body and move it along this path in the same direction. After repeating this a few times, close your eyes and again practice sending out energy with your imagination. Continue this for at least five minutes. Through this simple breathing method, all the resentment or frustration built up in your chest will just melt away.

Revitalizing Meditation

If you often feel fatigued and languid in the afternoon or if you somehow lack energy and feel weary, try Magnetic Meditation for vitalizing body and mind. For recharging your vitality, it's good to activate your first and second chakras together.

The first chakra is located between the genitals and the anus, and it is where dynamic, pure life energy gathers. If your first chakra is healthy, you overflow with vitality, strength, and gusto for life. If this location is blocked, however, you lack vigor and vitality, and have trouble lifting your eyes when you're around people.

The second chakra is located about two inches below the navel, and it is the energy center in our bodies where the most energy gathers. If your second chakra is activated, you give off a great vitality, but if it's not, you easily feel tired and also lack ambition in life.

As the sources of physical vitality, the first and second chakras are very closely interconnected, and if you activate one, the other is activated, too.

Tapping the Lower Abdomen
with a Magnet

Holding an Energy Magnet in each hand, use them alternately to tap your lower abdomen. In particular, focus on tapping your second chakra, the area about two inches below your navel. Since the magnet has weight, this will feel heavier than when you do it with empty hands. Tap your belly for at least five minutes. You'll feel a pleasant sense of heat in your lower abdomen.

Hold an Energy Magnet sideways in the fingers of each hand with the tips of the magnets facing each other and use them to make little circles in front of your first chakra. Imagine that the magnetic field generated by the magnets is activating the energy field of your first chakra. Repeat this movement for two to three minutes. You'll feel a sense of heat, magnetism, or gentle vibration in the area around your genitals and hips.

Activate your second chakra using the same method as you used with your first chakra. Imagine that the magnetic field generated by the magnets is strengthening the energy field of your lower abdomen. Feelings of heat, magnetism, and vibration will occur around your lower abdomen and lower back. Another method for strengthening your second chakra is to touch your second chakra directly with the magnet or to make small circles with a slight distance between the magnet and your belly. You can use whichever method is most appropriate for you, or use all three methods.

Once you feel that your second chakra has been activated to a certain degree, hold the magnets with your fingers so that the ends point toward your abdomen, then use them to draw a vortex from the center of your belly outward, ensuring that a magnetic field surrounds your lower abdomen and hips. Next, touch the tips of the magnets to your second chakra and do anal sphincter contractions.

Breathe as you normally do. When you contract your anal sphincter, do it with the feeling that you are tightly closing the muscles, as if you're trying not to pass gas or holding back a bowel movement. After counting silently to yourself from one to five, relax your anal sphincter, which will return to normal. The point of this exercise is to flex only the anal sphincter, without forcing tension in your lower abdomen and thighs. When you do this for the first time, begin with thirty repetitions in one set, and then increase this to 100 repetitions when you're comfortable with the exercise.

Your head will become clearer and your belly warmer if you do anal sphincter contractions regularly. You will also have good digestion because your intestines will be exercised naturally. You'll develop concentration and perseverance, and your endurance will also improve. This is very effective, especially for revitalization and strengthening stamina.

Healing Time with a Partner

You can have pleasant healing moments with family or friends by using magnets to strengthen each other and soothe tired bodies and minds. The person receiving healing can sit or lie on the floor or sit in a chair. He or she can receive healing most comfortably while lying on the floor. Avoid uncomfortable hardness or cold when lying on the floor by first spreading out a blanket or yoga mat.

To help heal another person, apply the different solo methods of Magnetic Meditation to them. Most importantly, keep an attitude of care and concern for each other and fully accept that all life is connected through a single energy. Those doing the healing share energy with love and devotion; those receiving the healing accept their energy with a grateful heart. Also try switching roles. After the healing is done, take some time for communication and compassion as you talk with each other about what you felt.

First, the person doing the healing holds a magnet so that it points toward the body of the person receiving the healing. Keeping the magnet about one to two inches from the other person's body, gently sweep from the top of the head past the face and chest to the lower abdomen, from the chest past the shoulders, elbows, and wrists to the fingertips, and from the hips past the knees and ankles to the tips of the toes. As you do this, imagine that the stagnant energy that has accumulated in the other person's energy field is leaving his or her body.

This time, holding the magnet about one to two inches from the other person's chest, slowly draw a vortex from the center to the outside of her body, strengthening her energy field. Next, use the same method to make a vortex from the center to the outside of the person's lower abdomen, and then move to her forehead, expanding her energy field. When healing, it's most effective to first open the chest to make the person's heart and mind comfortable, and then move toward the lower abdomen and the head.

Now, as if wrapping the other person's body in an energy coil, move the magnet in coiling lines from the top of her head to the tips of her toes, sheathing her entire body in a magnetic field. Also create energy fields for her arms and legs using the same method. The energy of life flowing in your body is transmitted to the other person through the magnet, and you are using that power to cover her in a healing field of energy. Slowly and devotedly wrap her entire body, from head to toe, as if you were wrapping her up with bandages of energy. You may feel the other person's energy field becoming one with your own.

Now empty your mind and let your hands move as they will. When you concentrate and trust your consciousness completely to the feeling of energy, your hands will move as they see fit and send energy to the parts of the other person's body that need it. This sensitivity is not only found only in people who have practiced meditation or healing for a long time. Anyone can naturally uncover and use the sense of life innate within us all, if they believe their own energy sense and trust their body to use it.

Hold an Energy Magnet in your hand and place it directly against the other person's lower abdomen. After holding this position for about one minute, use the magnet to make small circles for about two to three minutes, keeping a slight distance between the magnet and the other person's body. Both those receiving and doing the healing will likely feel powerful energy. Use the same method to heal the other person's chest and forehead, too. Take more time, about five minutes, to perform healing on the other person's belly, chest, or forehead, wherever it is needed most; follow your own feeling or ask the person where they would like to receive energy.

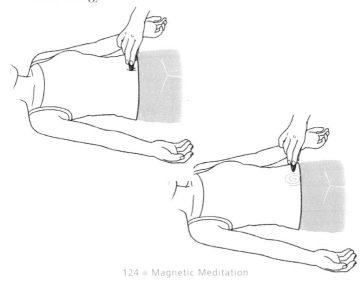

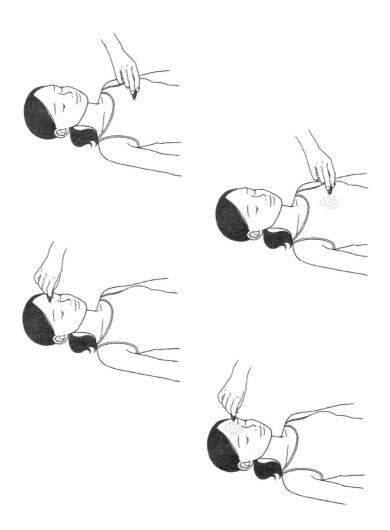

The person receiving the healing lies facedown on the floor. The person doing the healing holds a magnet in her fingers and uses its end to lightly and evenly tap on the other person's shoulders, upper back, and lower back. You can use one magnet or two, holding one in each hand. Using one magnet, either its end or its body, evenly massage the other person by lightly pressing or kneading as you make circles. Afterward, lift the magnet one to two inches from the other person's body and make small, spiraling circles, starting at the neck and moving down along the line of the spine to the lower back. Repeat this movement about three times.

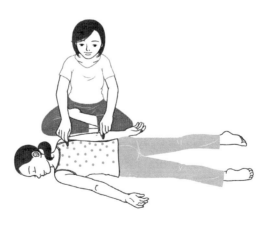

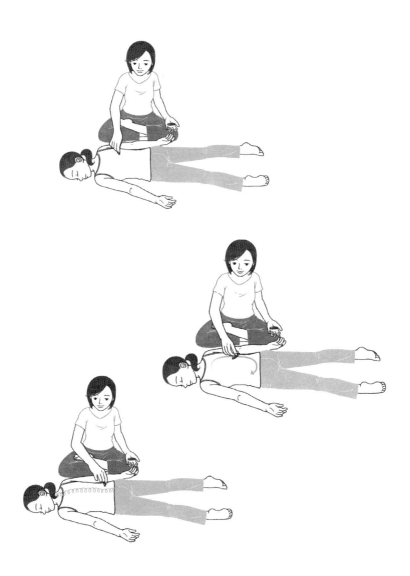

Charge the other person with energy by holding the end of the magnet for about one to three minutes on the middle point of the spine, located opposite the chest. Energize her lower back and tailbone in the same way. It's also helpful just to place a magnet on these spots without touching them with your hand.

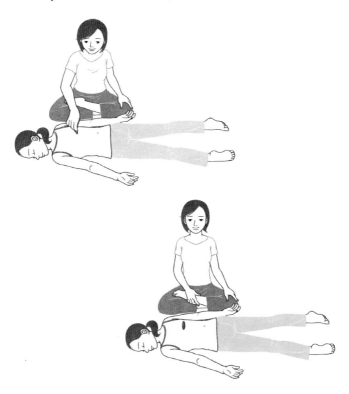

Five Minutes of Daily Healing
Using a Magnet

Acupressure is one of many tools based on the energy principles of Oriental medicine that can be easily used to support a healthy lifestyle. It is a method for invigorating the circulation of blood and energy that involves pressing meridian points lightly with the hand, instead of using a needle.

The ends of the Energy Magnets are very effective for acupressure because they are round and pointed. There is no limit to what you can do with a magnet if you have sufficient knowledge of the meridians and meridian points as they relate to the organs of the human body. Even learning a few of the most basic meridian points helps greatly.

It doesn't matter if you don't know any meridian points at all, however. Everyone instinctively covers or massages with their hands specific parts of the body where they feel pain or discomfort. If you have places that feel stiff or unwell, try using the end of a magnet to lightly tap, gently press, or softly massage them. Doing this with devotion for just five minutes is effective.

The following are basic meridian points that help alleviate light symptoms people commonly suffer. Doing this with family and friends is helpful because you grow to have more interest in each other's health, and you can talk together naturally about different things.

For Headache

Gently tap your whole head with the tip of a magnet, and then massage or gently press the Baekhwe point at the crown of your head with a magnet, the Taeyang points on your temples, and the Pungji points located on both sides of the back of your head in indentations along the boundary where your hair grows.

For Eye Fatigue

Stimulate the Indang point located in the indentation right above the point between your eyebrows, the Taeyang points in both of your temples, and the places right below where your eyebrows begin.

For a Cold

Stimulate your Pungji points and Daechu point, which is located where your neck bones stick out when you bend your neck forward.

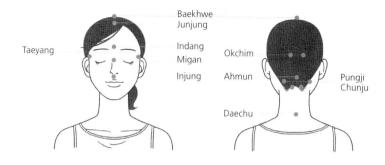

Taeyang

Baekhwe
Junjung

Indang
Migan

Injung

Okchim

Ahmun

Daechu

Pungji
Chunju

For a Stiff Neck

Massage and gently press with the tip of the magnet the area along the boundary where your skin and hair meet at the back of your neck. In particular, stimulate the Pungji points and the Gokji points. To locate a Gokji point, bend your elbow while holding your arm in front of your body. The point is found in the concave spot where the bone of your upper arm meets the two bones of your lower arm on the side facing away from your body. You have one Gokji point on each arm.

For Painful Shoulders

Stimulate the Gyeonjeong points, which are located at the point where a line coming up from the nipples intersects the line of the shoulders on the upper part of the shoulders. It's also good to stimulate the Pungji and Gokji points, as well.

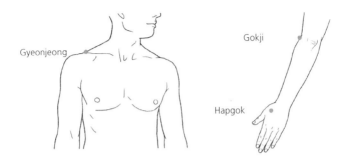

Gyeonjeong

Gokji

Hapgok

For a Bloated Stomach

Stimulate the Hapgok point, which is located between the finger and thumb in the part that protrudes most when you touch your thumb to your index finger, and the Taechung point, which is located at a spot about a half inch up the back of your foot from the place between your big toe and second toe.

For Trouble Sleeping

Stimulate the Baekhwe point on the crown of your head, the Taeyang points in both temples, and the Sameumgyo points, which are located on a spot about the distance of three finger widths up from your ankle bone on the inside of your shin. Pressing forcefully on the center of your palms also helps.

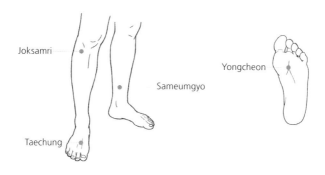

Gently press and knead the entire sole of your foot with the tip and body of a magnet. Stimulate the Yongcheon point, which is located in the concave spot that forms when you curl your toes, about one-third of the way down from the top of your foot, excluding your toes.

Stimulate the Joksamri point, which is located in a spot about three finger widths down from the knee on the outer part of the shin. Firmly press with a magnet over the entire soles of your feet and massage them by pressing gently or kneading them.

Gently tap the affected areas with the end of a magnet or gently knead them with the tip or body of the magnet. Or, lie with your back on the floor and rest comfortably for about five minutes with magnets placed on your chest and lower abdomen or in the palms of your hands. Placing too many magnets on your body could make you dizzy, so it's best not to put more than two magnets on your body at once. After you're done, slowly standup and gently shake out your arms and legs.

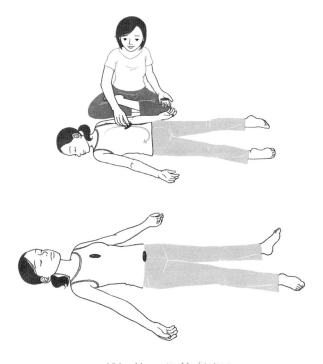

Magnet Hand Exercises for Awakening Brain Sensitivity

German philosopher Immanuel Kant said, "The hand is the visible part of the brain." Scientists believe that exquisite hand movements played a decisive role in human evolution and brain development. Thirty percent of the motor and sensory centers in the brain are said to be used for moving the hands. About one-fourth of a person's 206 bones are in the hands. This tells us how much we depend on the sensitivity and flexibility of our hand movements.

We make complex tools and create beautiful works of art with our hands, and we can feel subtle tactile sensations, thanks to the nerve endings concentrated in the tips of our fingers. When the power suddenly goes out, and we are left in the dark where our eyes, our most important sensory organs, cannot perform their proper role, we all instinctively feel our way through the darkness with our hands.

Industrious hands make a creative brain. The more

we move our hands, and the more frequently, the better. The more vigorously we move our hands, the more our brains develop along with them. When I was young, elders in my home village in Korea would put two walnuts in each hand, rolling them around with a clacking sound. This is a wise approach to healthy living, providing both hand exercise and stimulating the meridian points in the palms, which can help prevent dementia.

You can also use magnets to do a variety of hand exercises that develop your hands' motor sensitivity and stimulate their meridian points. Additionally, by playing games with your children, like the ones you did when you were very young, you can enjoy having a youthful mind and reminisce about your childhood, too.

Hold one to three magnets in your hands and alternately squeeze and relax them, as if you were kneading a lump of bread dough. Repeat these motions as you continue to roll the magnets with your thumb. This is effective for evenly stimulating the meridian points in the palms of your hands.

Hold two to three magnets in your hands and use your fingers to move one of the magnets above or below the others one at a time. Another method is to rotate one magnet at a time 180 degrees using your fingers. Magnets usually make a clacking sound when they hit each other, but try to move them so that they don't make any sound if possible. You'll develop greater concentration, and the movements of your hands will become much finer.

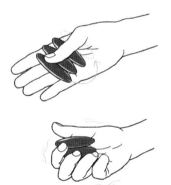

Playing Magnet Marbles

This is like a game of marbles you might have played when you were young. Lay out many magnets with lots of space between them. Flick one magnet with your fingers so that it sticks to another magnet. Keep doing this until all of the magnets are stuck together. As they stick together, the magnets make interesting sounds and pop into the air. Try to use many different movements, as you may have done when playing marbles as a child.

Magnetic Meditation: Applications ● 139

Although it's difficult to call these movements "hand games," they are exercises that simultaneously activate hand and eye coordination, and left and right brain function, so they have the effect of killing three birds with one stone, so to speak. Hold a magnet with the thumb, index, and middle finger of your right hand and extend your arm forward. With your eyes fixed on the magnet, spend five minutes slowly drawing the symbol for infinity in the air. Also, try drawing the infinity symbol in the opposite direction. The pupils of your eyes should follow the magnet. Also try switching your hands.

Easing Tinnitus in My Ears
Crispin Sargent, Denver, Colorado

I am a Dahn Yoga practitioner and just celebrated my tenth year of practice. Over the years, I have come to appreciate its healing modalities and the many tools it provides for our own healing and for sharing with others.

I first experienced the effect of magnets at a lecture Ilchi Lee gave at a workshop. He gave all two hundred of us bullet-sized magnets, and I put them by my ears because I had been experiencing tinnitus. For the last two or three years, I had heard unexplained buzzing and felt pressure in my ears. The buzzing in my ears got louder whenever I was stressed or tired or when the noise around me increased. Often this led to pressure headaches because I was trying so hard to hear through the buzzing.

As soon as I placed the magnets near my ear, the buzzing and pressure and noise around me became balanced, and I did not have to struggle as much to hear. When I returned to my home in Denver, I happened to acquire a set of small, square magnets. I started wearing them every day, especially whenever my mind needed to quiet down.

The magnets lessen the vibration and pressure, so now I don't get headaches. They are a great tool for quieting my mind. When I put the magnets on a stress point, such as at the upper, round part of my ear, I become calmer and more centered. That feeling stays with me even after I take off the magnets. The effect of the magnets helps me do other forms of meditation more easily, especially in classes and workshops that involve a lot of people and noise.

I also spend a lot of time in my car visiting clients as part of my job as a geriatric care manager. That's my thinking time. So I tend to put them on in the car. I generally have them on for about two hours a day. It helps me deal with stress, or traffic noise, or whatever I'm experiencing. I've never looked for a quick fix or a magic bullet, but the magnets worked right away.

An Amazing Meditation Tool

Jinhui Kim, Seoul, South Korea

One day, I came across Magnetic Meditation at a meditation center. The center was developing a variety of programs for developing the concentration of elementary school students using magnets. Actually experiencing it for myself, I found that the elementary school program had a variety of games and energy experiences for becoming familiar with magnets. Perhaps that's why I hadn't thought of it as a meditative method. I thought that it would be a good tool for people who have trouble feeling energy or for beginning meditators. I didn't think it would be helpful for me because I'm an avid meditation practitioner who has experienced diverse methods of meditation.

My thinking totally changed, though, when I tried using magnets as meditative tools for myself. The feeling was very powerful. I found it to be truly effective for purifying the energy state of my body and mind, as well as for filling myself with energy. Magnetic Meditation brought me great changes in just three days. Below is a simple summary of those feelings.

Day One

I did 33 prostrations, a form of meditation that I always enjoy, moved my body a little, and did brain exercises. And, sitting comfortably, I placed a magnet in the very center of my palms and breathed for a moment. As the centers of my palms grew very hot, I felt heat and energy all over my palms. I then immediately got the feeling that energy was filling my whole body. I sat breathing only for a moment, but, just through that small difference of holding a magnet, my body felt light all day.

Day Two

A little fatigued and aching all over, I didn't hesitate to grab some magnets, thinking that I needed an energy boost. I tapped my lower abdomen with my fists for about five minutes and did Brain Wave Vibration, a form of dynamic meditation. Of course, my fists each held a magnet. Continuing, I opened my hands and let the magnets resting in each palm, which I held in place with my thumbs. Then raised my hands to chest height and held them so that my palms faced each other. I then concentrated on the energy of the magnets as I repeatedly moved my hands closer together and farther apart. I imagined that my chest was filling with energy and opening up and my feelings of tiredness and frustration were draining away. I trained as if there was a door in my chest and as if that door was opened and closed automatically by the energy of the magnets. How much had I concentrated? My lower abdomen and chest seemed to be connecting when I heard a whirring sound in my once-tense brain, which started to feel cooler and relieved. I heard what sounded like raindrops falling as a relaxed feeling spread at the back of my neck, which had been stiff. Also, my left nostril, which would get stuffed up whenever I didn't feel good, opened up. After doing Magnetic Meditation in this way, my lower abdomen was full of energy all day, so I focused well and felt refreshed.

Day Three

Developing confidence in the effectiveness of Magnetic Meditation, I resolved to try focusing on it. I did three prostrations slowly, got my balance, and sat up straight. I placed one magnet in each of my palms and concentrated on the crown of my head. I imagined my crown opening and energy circulating throughout my body, and I visualized the magnets in the palms of my hands amplifying that energy for me. As the feeling of magnetism gradually grew stronger in my palms, I felt energy entering and leaving my body through the centers of my palms every time I breathed; it was as if my palms were breathing. It seemed as if my whole body was being connected by a single energy, as if my body were a magnet, and my crown felt cooler and also lighter.

By the time I ended my training, my body felt lighter and seemed to be filled with energy like a charged battery. I had a lot of hard work that day, but I had no trouble taking care of it thanks to Magnetic Meditation.

Magnetic Meditation allowed me to feel energy more powerfully than any other method of meditation I have experienced. When I did Magnetic Meditation with all the children in my class, it seemed to create a strong magnetic field that filled the classroom. It felt as if, with the magnets, each part of my body was being powerfully connected with the others by a single magnetic field.

Franklin Hughes, Sedona, Arizona

I got my first hint of the possibilities of using magnetic items to assist in my meditation some months ago when I joined an outside hiking/meditation group. This was in Sedona, a place I'm lucky enough to live in, and our group had gathered close to Bell Rock. This positive event led me on my way to exploring magnetism and magnetic meditation more fully.

I teach a yoga/meditation class at the Sedona Meditation Center on Friday nights. Some of the members are beginners, just delving into the idea of energy and meditation. So I thought that I would try to use magnets to help them better understand one of the ways that they can feel energy. When we got to the meditation portion of the evening, the first exercise we tried was to have them hold one magnet in each hand and slowly rotate their hands, something like having a dish or a really big donut between their hands. Of course, when the magnets were close to each other, they could feel a very strong alternating pull and push as they rotated their hands. Then I asked them to slowly move their hands further apart while rotating them. The sense one feels at the point where your hands are approximately one foot apart is quite a bit weaker, but still very apparent. Some could even feel the pull and repulsion when their hands were even further apart. This I told them was one of the ways that they would feel energy between their palms, even without the magnets.

Next, we put the magnets down and tried to just feel our natural energy. The experience of using the magnets as a learning tool allowed every single person to feel their own energy.

Then, I divided them up into pairs and gave two magnets to each person. First, I had one hold the magnets in their open palm, face up (with eyes closed), and I had the other person slowly rotate their magnets over the other person's hands. As we had an uneven number of people in the class, I also did this with one of the attendees. Of course, everyone with the open palms could feel this movement in their magnets; a very unusual feeling, like something alive in your hands. Then I had the person who was moving the magnets put them down on the floor, away from everything, and just open their hands, palm down, facing their partner's palms and slowly rotate their empty palms over the other person's stationary palms that still had magnets lying in them. I heard little gasps from the others (and even from myself). I couldn't believe how powerful the energy was between my partner's and my hands. Somehow, the magnets were acting as an amplifier or magnifier. I had never felt another person's energy so powerfully in my own palms. Sometimes, I guess, it's good to astonish the teacher along with the students. The feeling I received was one of sharing loving, peaceful energy with my partner—a feeling of compassion, yet strength that tied us together.

Magnets can help amplify one's own natural energy and open up the senses, a wonderful tool to use.

Eungi Bang, Seoul, South Korea

I'm an early adopter of IT devices. As I actively made use of IT devices for work, I was able to achieve many things easily in a short time. I found out, however, that this habit had significant side effects. Concentrating on the screen for long hours often made my eyes dry and easily bloodshot. What is more, I developed symptoms of so-called "military neck" from long hours of PC use, and my neck and shoulder pain became chronic. Living attached to a mouse and smart phone often left me with painful, stiff wrists. Whenever I got signs of abnormality in my body, I tried massaging it, I tried tapping it, and I tried meditating, but I had trouble concentrating, and pain that would disappear for a short time would soon come back.

During this time, quite by accident, it was suggested to me that I try Magnetic Meditation. The word magnet made me think of the tools we used to learn north and south polarity during school science classes or the things we use to stick memos on a refrigerator. Doing meditation with those magnets seemed a bit odd to me. Much to my surprise, though, directly experiencing Magnetic Meditation actually gave me regrets: "Why didn't I know about this before?!"

If I were to describe in my own way the greatest advantage of Magnetic Meditation, it would be the depth, intensity, and speed of the meditation. These effects help both beginners who are coming across meditation for the first time, as well as people who have some degree of familiarity with meditation. Although you can do meditation without magnets, using magnets allows you to concentrate easily and quickly. What beginning meditators have the hardest time with is emptying their minds of distracting thoughts. With Magnetic Meditation, you can easily gather your awareness because the magnets have their own energy. So it's a great method for beginners.

That's not all. It leads longtime meditators into a deeper meditative state. With Magnetic Meditation, I was easily able to experience deep, profound states of consciousness and energy that even I—proud though I am as a longtime meditator—have rarely experienced without magnets.

The greatest change that has happened in my life as I've done Magnetic Meditation is that I now have one more friend in my life full of IT gadgets—magnets. Meditation, they say, is about learning how to play well with one's self. Even with all my experience, I don't think I've actually experienced for myself the truth of those words. Since I've been doing Magnetic Meditation, though, I've been fully experiencing how fun and fascinating it is to play with my body.

Since my wife Fran had her stroke five years ago, we have tried many types of therapy, from physical therapy to acupuncture to water therapy. Nothing has really worked at all. Now that she is in class at a Dahn Yoga center, there have been several advancements in her well-being. The most notable happened because of Magnet Meditation—she is starting to use her right hand and arm, and it's only been a few short weeks! I use the magnets too, on my arthritic fingers and toes.

Morrie Puzzi, Scottsdale, Arizona

Magnetic Meditation is so powerful that I think it won't be easy to find a better way to revive a weak energy sense. When I continued to hold magnets in my hands and touch them, I found that the sensitivity of my hands revived and became stronger. What's more, the strong magnetism causes the energy to enter my wrists, arms, and even my shoulders, as well as my hands. I think it would be very good for improving manual dexterity in elderly people, especially. I plan to give the gift of magnets to my mother, who is in a nursing home, and to teach her how to do Magnetic Meditation, too.

Meg Robinson, Austin, Texas

I know immediately the condition of my mind and body when I do Magnetic Meditation. Holding a magnet above my body and moving it down across my whole body, as if scanning it, I can tell where fatigued organs or stiff muscles are. I do Magnetic Meditation also when I'm under a lot of stress or feeling bad about something. In front of my chest, I hold a magnet in each hand, and, spreading my hands apart when I inhale and moving them together when I exhale, I move the magnets with my breathing. When I do this, I feel the frustration and constriction in my chest dissipating, and my breath sinking to my lower abdomen.

Pamela Kelley, Baltimore, Maryland

I really want to recommend Magnetic Meditation to people who have trouble with circulation in their bodies. The powerful magnetism of the magnets seems to activate the magnetism flowing in our bodies, facilitating circulation throughout. Because of this, it's a really good tool, especially for healing and massaging the body. I press and massage my head with the magnet when my head hurts, the soles of my feet anytime I'm sitting down, and my chest when I have frustrating, constricted feelings in my chest, which clears up unpleasant feelings.

Steve Chen, Fort Lee, New Jersey

I have been using all types of magnets in my meditation classes at the Body + Brain Center in Smithtown, New York. We do activities such as putting two magnets together and using another to make them move in a circle and putting one magnet in each hand and circling them around each other while feeling the magnetic sensation. We even took turns using them on each other. Using the magnets allows my students to experience a relaxed mental state without thoughts. It's so exciting to see their minds become so centered and clear. One person even saw colors as well. I feel that this hand-on approach to meditation will promote change faster in people because they can feel it, see it, and even hear it.

Tamia Bethea, Smithtown, New York

I have long done meditation training, but, even when meditating, it has been difficult to concentrate when I'm under great stress or my condition has declined. I've found, though, that my concentration definitely increases when I do meditation with magnets. The magnetism is strong, so I concentrate easily and am not bothered by distractions, either. I recommend it to people who want to take some time alone to meditate, even if for moment, in their busy lives.

Phil Coleman, Palo Alto, California

Afterword

As we live our lives, we find that there are times when maintaining balance is difficult. There are times when, unbeknown to us, we lean too much to one side, lose our balance, and almost fall. "Uh-oh!" we say. In the moment we get that feeling, we should quickly wake up and pay attention, and rediscover that absolute, impartial center within ourselves. We must recover the eyes of an observer so that we are able to see everything as it is, which brings harmony, balance, and creative order to our lives.

The secret that makes this possible is the ability to feel the energy that flows in, around, and between all life. When we feel that energy, the current of life flows freely in and around our bodies, and we breathe deeply. "Uh-oh" becomes "Ahhh!" as we let go of our stresses. Our troublesome thoughts quiet down, and our minds recover tranquility. Then we can finally say, "Aha!"

I composed this photo of a pine tree and rock while

playing around with magnets. They can maintain these forms without losing their balance, even though they look unstable and likely to collapse, because of the pushing and pulling force operating between them.

The same power underlies our lives in the world. This power exists not only in my own body, but between me and other people, between humans and other life-forms, and, perhaps more importantly, between the Earth and all life. Consequently, developing sensitivity for maintaining balance and harmony in all those re-lationships—with their ceaseless opening and closing, pushing and pulling—is very important work that ben-efits all life, not just me as an individual.

I hope you will play and meditate with the magnets whenever you get the chance, and that, as you do this, you will develop your sense for energy and will practice a lot using energy. I believe that in this process you will naturally come to understand more deeply the principles that move our bodies, our minds, and the world. The greater our experience and understanding of energy grows, the more our sense for life revives, and we discover a direction for a meaningful life that is considerate of ourselves, others, and all life.

Acknowledgements

I would like to acknowledge Dahyang Lee and Junghwa Kang in organizing and editing the material from my lectures and workshops. I would also like to express my gratitude to Daniel Graham for translating my words from Korean to English. Thanks are also due to the staff of BEST Life Media for their constant support in shaping this book through all of its stages.

Resources

If you want to learn more about simple and easy ways to manage and balance your energy like Magnetic Meditation, visit www.changeyourenergy.com.

Conceived by Ilchi Lee, this online hub for integrative lifestyle education provides online classes and courses, workshops and retreats, and private coaching and group training that facilitate positive changes for individuals and groups.

This website can work as the primary source of tools, resources, and support for those who desire to create positive changes in their lives, share the idea of change with others, and make a difference in their communities.

About the Author

Ilchi Lee is an impassioned visionary, educator, mentor, and innovator; he has dedicated his life not only to teaching energy principles, but also to researching and developing methods to nurture the full potential of the human brain.

For over thirty years, his life's mission has been to empower people and to help them harness their own creative power and personal potential. To help individuals achieve that goal, he has developed many successful mind–body training methods, including Dahn Yoga and Brain Education. His principles and methods have inspired many people around the world to live healthier and happier lives.

Lee is a New York Times bestselling author who has penned thirty-six books, including *The Call of Sedona: Journey of the Heart, Healing Society: A Prescription for Global Enlightenment*, and *Brain Wave Vibration: Getting Back into the Rhythm of a Happy, Healthy Life.*

He is also a well-respected humanitarian who has been working with the United Nations and other organizations for global peace. Lee serves as the president of the University of Brain Education and the International Brain Education Association.

For more information about Ilchi Lee and his work, visit www.ilchi.com.